AF230805

Vernacular

Vernacular

Vernacular the album is available to purchase and stream on all good streaming outlets.

Direct link: *http://hyperurl.co/qwyh6r*
Merchandise and contact: *www.theorator.bigcartel.com*
Mailing list sign up: *www.eepurl.com/ciAZBD*

Social media:
Twitter: *@TheOrator_UK*
Instagram : *@TheOrator_UK*

Best place to catch a live show?
Anywhere. Everywhere. Otherwise, see above.

Acknowledgments

Let it be known that this work exists primarily for those who needed it most when they stumbled upon it. Many thanks are owed to the village of Manduar, The Gambia for welcoming me so warmly when putting this book together. I thank the most high for the sun. Thank you to the people that inspired me, wished me well, motivated me, asked me to live their dreams for them and those who told me 'don't stop, we need that narrative ·.

Love.

Thank you to Hanane Belaroussi for the beautiful interpretations of ten selected poems within the book. Ten original hand-painted images lie between the covers of this book, we thank Belaroussi for this.

Thank you to lrfan Chhatbar for all design work that bought my words to life on the page. I further extend my gratitude to Mr. Chhatbar for the years of continued support for Rhetoric Literary Society and myself. Thank you sir.

Much love to all the supporters. You've enabled me to tick off life goals long before what my school teachers said the due date would be. For that, I've got you for life.

For:
Mum, Manshus, Kaylin, Aunty Jaq, Harlum, Zelina, Uncle Paul, Grandma, Big Grandma, Granddad, Dad, Dianne, Rekel, Duchess, Empress, Shafika, Cyrus, Jesse, Jermain and Renee. Family. Sam Zircon, Twisted Pennys, Bisk, Sam Grubb, dtp, Norman, Dr. Sallah, Naizer, Bobby Brown, Mono, Big Sam, Mr Camara, Jabang and Kabala.
Chikka, Yasin, Scrivs, Bobba Bennett, HQ Nick, Gra8755, everybody fighting fascists, reflecting love and Leicester, LESTA.

Contents

Section one

Let us walk

The Mystery of Poetic Brilliance.. 9
For Anybody That'll Listen... 10
Oh Ye Purveyor Of Fine Lies.. 11
De Pannekoekenboot.. 12
Dear Valencia.. 13
Displaced 14
Conversations With The Mind 15
Transcendence 17
Wildflowers 18
Bumblebee 18
Glisten 19
Inspire Me 20
Leap 22
Neither Here Nor There 23
The hills of Hanging Haughton.. 24
Spirit Gypsy.. 25
Winter In The City Of The Foxes... 26
Wood For Trees... 27

Section two
The idea of Love

Astro-Love.. 29
Divinity.. 32
The Empress Affirmation... 34
For Coloured Girls.. 37
Endure.. 39
Black Beauty... 40
Please Do Not Fuck With My Heart..................................... 42
Uncool... 44

All Men Are The Same.. 46
The Beautiful Affirmation.. 50
We Will... 51
Don't Blink.. 52
Ruzumble in The Juzungle of The Ventricle...................... 53
Goodbye My Lover.. 55
Back To Love... 58

Section three
Reflections

757... 60
Black Power Black Man... 61
A Cold Place.. 64
I See No Humour... 65
I Need Hope... 67
Henergy.. 70
My Fashion Is Black... 71
Free.. 73
Daddy's Going To Change The World.................................. 74
The Walk Alone... 75
Who Killed The Stereotype... 78
W.O.R.D.S... 81
The Smiling Coast... 83
Ode To MLK... 86
Madiba.. 88

Section one

Let us walk

The Mystery Of Poetic Brilliance

Confined to the pages of history

They will seldom call upon our brilliance

Etched into the face of blank pages, journals and walls

Will be the greatest stories told of all

Contemporary tales of war to triumphs in love

Our Characters do age, as anybody would

Yet their tales prevail in ink and Braille

Lest we hail the flare in which poets do dare

Write our history how no other could

For Anybody That'll Listen

This poem will not be heralded a master piece

This poem will not be praised by critics near or far

For my friend, this poem is merely a reflection of my heart

This poem will not inspire the start of imminent revolution

This poem will not begin to right the wrongs of a broken society
For my friend, this poem is to be whispered, no, muttered - quietly

This poem will not stop the United States of America scavenging the world for oil

Nor will it stop the British following them in to financially motivated unjust war

For this poem my friend is the voice of the poor

This poem does not contain what some claim is the definition of life
This poem will not make the woman I love think twice

For this poem and myself
Are a little too alike - abstract

In fact - this poem is an ode to life

Celebrating all who see the world through open eyes
This poem is the truth but this poem is too a lie

This poem

Isn't and was never meant to be a poem

Simply the excretion of thoughts victim to my uncanny reason

This poem

Just is

Oh Ye Purveyor Of Fine Lies

Oh ye, purveyor of fine Lies

Why hide?

Though you dress it in fine guise

A percentile of the wise

Will not be fooled when you seek to have us believe

That the truth is in fact a Lie

Oh ye, purveyor of fine Lies

De Pannekoekenboot

The forces that be kiss my naked skin

They do so but ever so gently

As the elements wrap themselves around my being

I am engulfed by serenity

Winged machines interrupt the moments of stillness with their thunderous
engines

Their interruption is brief and the tranquility soon sets it's gaze back upon my
lonely being

Buildings whimper and wiggle there way across the jagged knife edge of ripples

Only to then trickle away into the depths of my moonlight perception

Were they ever even there?

Retinas scan for any tell tale signs of lands edge

Instead, they set on a flurry of distant lights

That flicker into and out of existence

Their rebirth humble not bright

But lest they remind us of beauty, and it's simplicity

Even, at the end of life

Dear Valencia

A swift breeze on the back of my neck

The sea creeps to the soles of my feet

The debris from lands foreign litters the dusty beaches

Beauty at its pinnacle

Oh how I wish I need not leave it

Displaced

With out roots I weep

From the balls of my feet

As the spirit is displaced

Pyrrhonism is all their remains to embrace

Conversations With The Mind

Would you be so kind as to allow me to spend some time with my mind?

There are a few things I have to get off my chest so it's best we speak now

I am tired of your obsession with the future

Everything we do, is done with a future daughter or son, in mind

Like, why?

We will get to that point in due time

So why can't we just focus on the now?

Enjoy the present for a bit

Maybe, be present for a bit

I am constantly in two places at one time

Possibly sat with you right now

Hearing every word you say

And still be a gazillion million miles away

I have every intention of hearing you speak

It's that mind thinks there's more interesting things

Like exploring thought

Creating and eclipsing the boundaries of reality

Coming up with the most awe-inspiring questions this universe has ever heard

Contemplating how the simple circle of life contains infinite complexities

Analysing ones self in real time as though the mind can detach itself running as

a parallel operating system so that it may envision

Vernacular

What's about to happen as it happens and so it happens it's happening right now

The world is shattering right now

Shattering

Right now

....There goes my mind again

The world is fine

Despite my mind seeing it fall flat in a million extravagant ways

I curse then I thank the universe for even giving me stay

If I don't reclaim it now I think my mind may run away

Away with the fairies

Scary

Or perhaps not

Every time I've gone to war with my mind, I've lost

Long before the battle begun

As soon as I went against it - it won

So from hence forth - I declare a truce

Mind - I am rolling with you

There'll be ups - there'll be downs

But its cool - I got you now

Run - Be free - Go mad

Because when they call us crazy - we'll dance

When they box us in - we'll sing

Because that's what makes us happy

And that's an important thing

Transcendence

Up with the birds

At the crack of dawn, I crack a yawn

And pen these words

The soul is a vessel

Carrying all that is good and all that is great

Links to ancestors

Maps of the universe and the power to elate

Travel through space wade through time

Converse with the gods, dance in the divine

All in your soul

All in your soul

Never sell your soul for what your body is worth in gold

Wildflowers

When hours become seconds

The wildflowers dwindle, long before their time

Forever becomes momentary; to blink would be a crime

The beauty of existence, is most certainly short liv**ed**

Bumblebee

To determine the direction of wind

You have to be among the trees

Humble among the bubble

Oh how I wish I were a bee

Glisten

Let your soul glisten

May your trials and tribulations

Be the catalyst in finding your

Internal eternal glow

The star shines day and night

But is only visible in the absence of light

Take heed

For one day you might

Have to show a person in need

Where they can find

Their internal eternal light

Inspire Me

Inspire me!

Isn't that what education's about?

Intellectuals and books

Mathematic and geometry and blowing things up

Inspire me!

Isn't that what education's about?

Well yes, and no

See the thing is bro

And sisters in attendance

Schooling and education are two completely different things

Schooling stops at 20 odd whereas education is then yet to begin!

The schooling versus education debate - such a wonderful thing

See, I remember a time when I was a likkle likkle yute

Forward and brazen - I admit it was true

Me and Mr Panford didn't get along; I thought he was an arrogant fool

But his daughter was peng so his bullshit I got used to

Until one day I challenged him, in front of the class

It was a genuine question - I wasn't just 'showing my ass'

As my mum would say

Inspire me!

Isn't that what education's about?

Reclaim your natural mind

It was once said that your schooling should not interfere with your education

Make every effort to ensure that it doesn't

Because schools churn out clones and it's blatant

Suppressing creativity in order to promote submissiveness

This frivolous system is most certainly mistaken

If they believe we will not be reclaiming our education

Reclaiming our creativity

Reclaiming our right to an open mind

We hereby request that we are no longer led by the blind

But the cool

The kids who didn't do too well in school

However could still teach you a thing or two

About business, arithmetic and chemistry too

We the generation new

Demand truth

Demand power to the people

Demand the right to be equal

Demand the right to knowledge so lethal

Inspire me!

Isn't that what education's about?

Leap

Stretch!

Tickle the stars

Find balance on the very tips of your toes

Yell!

Until the cows come home

Squint

As glistening rivers of joyous tears flow from saturated glands

This is your moment

Fly as though you never plan to land

Elation is at hand

Neither Here Nor There

On occasion I am elsewhere
Neither here nor there
Yet I am around
Sat next to you right now
Seeking something yet to be found
Listening tentatively
To all that surrounds
I am neither here nor there

Vacating with the fairies
Singing with canaries
Dancing a dance of joy
One foot here, one foot there
I am neither here nor there

On occasion I am very much elsewhere
Neither here nor there
But I'm local
Sat behind you on a bus
On journey so noble
Basking in the musk
Admit it though, one must
I am neither here nor there
Reasoning with the muse
Excavating truth

Remove the veil from your eyes
For on occasion I am elsewhere
Neither here neither there

The hills of Hanging Haughton

Just past Hanging Haughton

There's a place where angels sing

Where the sun it meets the earth

And it's rays doth kiss land's skin

Seas of green and waves of crop

Show the land is fertile

Such beautiful place is hard to find

Thank god that I got lost

Spirit Gypsy

When the mind wonders

The spiritual compass will be your guide

Open yourself to universal energy

See the world beyond your eyes

Winter In The City Of The Foxes

Long nights, cold days

The occasional spot of heavy rain

Fleeces and jumpers and big puffy coats

Oh how we wait for the first sign of snow

Wood For Trees

We know, it glows

But no, that don't

Mean, it's gold

See the wood, for the trees

Natural hair, through the weave

Make not believe, remove the veil and see

Section two

The Idea of Love

Astro-Love

As I understand

Words will only ever get in the way

When you're trying to explain

Something so amazing

It could only be said to be from another plain

But you, you're beautiful

Whether it be the crack of dawn or the middle of the night

There's something in your eyes

That ignites something inside of me

It's so unusual

But you, you're so much more than the usual

This must be some form of Astro-Love

So let us forget about the earth bound words and feelings

When we're in the spiritual world and our bodies start the
talking

We are only known as the chatter bugs

There's something about your aura that makes me feel like I
just can't get enough

So when we mix the dark chocolate with the caramel and our
lips begin to touch

It can only ever be described as a sugar rush

So sweet

Now baby I'm about to go deep and sweep you off of your feet
with lines so ...

Cheap.

However these other brothers can't do it like me

Because I can show you that I love you with my clothes on

I respect you for who you are and it's that deep

It doesn't matter if your hair has a receipt

Or whether it is short or whether it is long

Whether you are in the right or you are in the wrong

You are mine

I cannot say I will feel this way until the day that I die

But for the foreseeable future

I do not just want or need

But I would like you by my side

Divinity

I recall a time when true love was divine
A time when your being and my soul were intertwined
In a tight type of tied knot not tied down with love
But tied in some form of metaphysical bond like the moon and the tide
Your eyes being the moon, drawing me ever closer to you
Your essence so smooth, a gate way to heaven
I cannot wait to arrive at your pearly gates
Mentally and physically prepared
I proceed to run my fingers through your hair
And fixate my gaze upon your face
Almost as if time were told to wait, we pause
Allow the moment to settle
Such spirit in fine fettle
We then wrestle
One another to the first flat surface
Becoming a human furnace
Upon our decent into love, lust and everything between beneath and above
The temperature around us surges
Now I can see your aura
All of this, before we have locked lips
Let alone removed the clothes from your back or slid the jeans from your hip
God makes no mistake so there are no mistakes about this
So shhhh ... you need not say a word
Lie back, and observe
How I accelerate your heart rate and unsettle your nerves
Introduce you to the heavens
And bring you right back down to earth
Goddess so divine

The Empress Affirmation

I am a woman

I am the moon, the earth and the skies

I am courage, I am strength, I am pride

I am love; I am Joy and the source of all life

I am gods gift to the world

For Coloured Girls

This is a poem is for coloured girls

Here I have a message from the Brothers

The righteous fathers and future fathers of your children

Your carers and your lovers

We just want you to know that we love you

We love you as we find you

We love you as you are

Big lips, big hips, potentially pickey hair

Dimples and wrinkles

Emotional bruises and physical scars

We, love you for who you are

So please, embrace that

There's no need for weave every two weeks

Especially if it's recycled

And those who are guilty know exactly what I mean

Same time, I beg you do please

Ease off the relaxer

More so if you've noticed your hairline is beginning to recede

Oh and box yourself if you find yourself wanting to use bleaching cream

Brothers love that milk and dark chocolate

Vernacular

But some of you sisters are more interested in looking like whipped cream

Don't lose what you blessed with

It's not me you should be vex with

I'm just passing on the message

Please do embrace your blackness

Your pickey hair, big bum, thick lips, round thighs and average to big tits

Make us brothers fall to our knees

When you mix all of the above

With some Anne Summers or Victoria's Secrets

We just cannot resist

So I insist

That you keep it black

Because that soul sister, down-to-ride with ya sister

Is so effing missed

Natural hair, less exposed skin, hoop earrings and many other things

We wish oh how we wish

Would replace all this artificial capital B Bullshit

We aren't saying go back in time

Just acknowledge there was a time

When you could be proud of the things that made you black

This denying your blessings by wearing a mask crap

Just doesn't do you justice

We, as the brothers

Think you're fineee

Without that

Endure

If all is fair in love and war

                    Then thin is the line between joy and pain

Though flesh is temporary

                    The memories forged will always remain

Black Beauty

Dark chocolate milk chocolate caramel skin afro
curly kinky hair

She has a slim thick healthy temple

With a free thinking motivated formidable mind

Physically emotionally spiritually strong

Endlessly unconditionally all loving

Physically emotionally spiritually strong

Endlessly unconditionally all loving

Please Do Not Fuck With My Heart

Please do not fuck with my heart

Because the cost of tireless trust is too high

A cost I cannot fathom nor afford is what you require

Trust, a trust to garner foundations for our love to stand tall

Tall enough to eclipse darkness

Then lift us beyond earthly realms to places known well by our ancestors but to our children now untold

A place of Laughter, Love and Life

A ticket to this place cannot be bought for any price

This place is called faith

Many do not rate this place because they cannot touch nor taste its richness

They confuse money with value and believe you require sight in order to witness its greatness but hear this

Faith is within every single one of us

In each breath, in each cell

Whether you be in the office or be in a cell

Faith is within you and will protect you from hell

Because hell, is here on earth

It is where tear is believed to be stronger than love

Where money is the greatest wealth

And health is a victim to man made drugs

And reason is met by ignorance resembling concrete reinforced earplugs

This place just does not give a fuck for love

So we let the powers that be continue to pull the wool over our tear filled eyes

Our minds scream at this screen of propaganda infused lies

Asking for our feet to stomp to rhythms felt deep in side

And our fists to rise

Rise until we reach the sky

And then continue

Past the ego, leaving behind all pride

Submerge yourself within me

As I will onto you

This is love true

Break the self-imposed chains of the norm

Your soul is more precious than gold, beautifully adorned

Naked as the day you were born

I love you as you so can you love me forever more?

Because I have faith in you

Perfect - the only word to describe how the most high created you

I only ask that you do not fuck with my heart

Uncool

Why is it uncool to fight for what you love?

We walk away from love too easily

We're scared if it's not easy

Careless in where we place it but reluctant to love freely

Why is it uncool to fight for what you love?

All Men Are The Same

I write this to evidence that all men are the same

We all play psychological games

Each in our own special way

We all only want thing

For that, there is no denying

We're manipulative

And in doing so, sometimes insensitive

We all find it hard to trust

Yet we know it's an integral part of being able to love

But hey, as you say, we're all players

It's not hard to see why so many women hate us

Frankly, we all like it easy

It shouldn't be a surprise, believe me

Because we're all the same right?

We may say

"Bae go play - enjoy your freedom"

Well secretly we all like to be controlling so regarding that

we' re only teasing

Because all men are the same

As we advance

I'll begin to explain why all men are the same

Before I conclude it'll be clear as a midsummers day

As to why I say

All men are the same

Number one:

We all play psychological games

True!

Because in order to figure out what the hell is going on inside

a woman's brain we have to

Number two:

We all only want one thing

And no, no, no - it's not sex

As happy as we get at the thought of you being undressed

We just want to be loved

Vernacular

Number three:

We're all manipulative

Now there's no getting around it

This act of treason we commit because history shows us

To stand a fighting chance of living happily ever after we have

to bend the rules a bit

Number four:

We all find it hard to trust

This one is simple

Women aren't the only ones capable of having their hearts and

souls crushed

Number five:

Every last one of us, is a grade 'A' player

We play this game and that game

The put up with your crap game

And still we can't win

Number six:

We all like it easy, don't you?

We're tired of being taken for a ride

Occasionally it gets boring being alone

So how would it feel if you got to know my every detail? Only to

be sent that way

To the friend zone

Finally Number seven:

We are all too controlling

And some of us are

It is no excuse but please tolerate the idea that some of us still

carry deep emotional scars

A thin line exists between being controlling and being

protective

Furthermore being protective is sometimes just who we are

So I agree

All men are the same

Question is

How many women out there will allow themselves to see it this

way?

The Beautiful Affirmation

Beauty

Is something they can never take away

Be strong in who you are

Don't let them tell you that you aren't

As beautiful as the sunrise that blesses the landscape every
morning of every day

Be strong in who you are

Beauty is something they can never take away

Now say

I'm beautiful

We Will

I will exercise the inside of your thighs

You will quiver, roll and squint your eyes

I will take you to places you thought existed only in your mind

You will sit and ride until your posture's realigned

I will thrust and jive till the sheets are soaked

We'll do every last thing you say you won't

I will stroke and dip between those buttercream hips

You'll shiver and drip down my base, neck and tip

We will

Oh how we will

Don't Blink

I guess what I'm saying is

Seize the day

Embrace everything for what it is

What's here now may be gone tomorrow

Irrespective of race creed and colour

Love waits for no one

Blink once and it could be gone

Ruzumble in The Juzungle of The Ventricle

Passion, Pain and Love

Most of us have felt all of the above

Few of us have felt all three simultaneously

However if you are one of the few

Give thanks for the situations you've lived through

Because - love kills

Those who love most passionately feel the most pain

So much so - it has the strength to drive a mad man sane

And the sane man to the grave

It may look splendid to untrained eye

Little do they know of its harmful ways

Love freely except be prepared for the cage

If you truly care, be aware of the rage

That comes when love gets tough

The other half just can't or won't do enough

You may find yourself searching for the answers and
questions unknown

Why is it always me?

Is true love destined only for the caucasian middle class family

with two kids and a Labrador?

You know the ones you see in the movies that always end

happily?

Stay hopeful, stay committed, stay focused and stay with it

As hard as it may be and as big as the associated risks are

It's all worth it when you make it through the dark

Nobody wants to die alone

But not many of us have the cojones to step in the ring

Knowing 12 rounds with the baddest roughest toughest most

awesome of a thing is waiting for you to go toe to toe

If you can do it

I salute you

And if you can come out on top

The rewards speak for themselves

Goodbye My Lover

That warm gaze from those hazel eyes

Is the fuse to what would be no more than a hollow space just left of my chest

With an exuberant finesse

You made sense of the spaghetti hoops of a mess

Which was once my life

You changed my entire outlook

Broke down my iron curtains

Thus replacing my fears

With feelings of elation

Connecting - not just in the bedroom

Equally as much through stimulating intellectual conversation

You are all which is good about the most highs creation

I stood trial against the test of time

And welcomed my position in the dock

Found guilty of irrational love

You, no other

Have my heart on lock

Vernacular

If there is any justice in the world

You would throw away the key

Refuse to set me free

Cuddle me close

As I hope forever you will be

With me

You were my everything

You are my everything

Wedding ring or no wedding ring

Till death do us part I sing

Till death do us part till death do us part

This is just the beginning

Of the end

Let us not pretend

This decision will not result in the collapse of worlds

Implosion of schema

Or bring about doubt to the most devout of believers

In love

If only I could change that which has already been written in the stars

If only I could rearrange the constellations so that my world would never know
of the dark

Owing to the fact that you

Would be the centre of my universe

Your radiance transcends all things known to men

Well, to this one at least

Don't go.

Come back.

Anything. Something.

Please

Back To Love

Like watching somebody put up an Ikea flat pack in reverse

My ideal world was disassembled

Rewriting the stories played over in my mental

Space was necessary for the essential

Act of picking myself up

Fuck.

This isn't how it was supposed to go

The very existence of this poem prevents the possibility of growth

But hey

You know - what will be will be

So for me it's possibly best I go

With the flow

For now anyway

I'll get back to love some day.

Section three

Reflections

757

As life is in peril

    And we peer over world's ledge

      Lest we forget

        The sheer beauty in death.

Black Power Black Man

Is it wrong for me to shout out Black Power?

Would you be offended if I proclaimed my blackness from the
rooftops?

On the hour every hour

Words raining down from the heavens like a harsh winter
shower

Falling on ignorant ears and open ears all the same

Indifferent to intolerance - Kuntah is my name

Don't you ever call me Toby

I am nobodies slave

Decimate my character

Spit upon my name

Reduce me to statistics

But you could never ever kill me

Regardless of your aim

One shot, two shot

Three shots aflame

The Black Man shall always remain

A Cold Place

Smile broad

Heart warm

To lose control

Is a loss I can't afford

Anger is an emotion

One I adorn

As with its power

To devour all

I See No Humour

'The Orator', they call

'You' re a man of great humour', they yell

Yet I see no humour in the blood rivers of the innocent

Nor in the souls of the 12 year old virgin militant

Who is unbeknown to a woman's sweet touch

And all too familiar with the cold hand grip of the Kalashnikov held firmly in his clutch

How can we expect humour in the absence of love?

Where's the humour in a six-year-old boy fending off his mothers abusive lover?

Six years old, no respect for fear just an innate instinct to protect his mother and brother

I can't see the humour

Is it funny to hear of the 16 year old couple

Who due to lack of support, due care and precaution

Are on to their 3rd abortion?

Or do you seek amusement in the unembellished accounts of female genital
mutilation?

Clitoridectomy and infibulation

Where is the joke?

Very little is funny from where I stand

By no means is it all bad

But I'm a big rarse man

And I get reduced to tears

When I see life long dreams disappear

Under the weight of mental chains and inordinate fears

Where is the jocularity in here?

When being in the wrong place at the wrong time can have you serving 25 to
life because of flaws in joint enterprise laws

I can't laugh any more than when I do when I contemplate how the west tried
to erase the history of the moors

This isn't my reality - it's yours

This isn't their suffering - it's ours

While some laugh easily

Others cry hard.

I Need Hope

They asked, how's life?

To which I replied, hard

I can't complain

In fact, I could, I probably should and would

I don't know, I need hope

Bailiffs came three times last week

I had to get back into bed

Pretend to be asleep under the sheets until they were gone

I need hope

I realized that I couldn't get a job

However, I have too much pride to sign on

These days you can't debate that crime pays

I need hope

My dreams were beginning to slip under the weight of every
day life

But I could never let them fade

The cost of failure is something I can't afford to pay twice

I need hope

I wanted a good woman

One not afraid to commit

I was ready and my heart is still legit

Lord knows I need hope

Not the biggest fan of religion

Although I've contemplated going to church

My faith in life is weak

It hurts

I need hope

I need hope. I need answers. I need faith. I need strength. I
need happiness. I need to feel a warm embrace. I need hope

There was no food in my cupboards, fridge or freezer

With two weeks till payday

Damn right I felt my strength getting weaker

I need hope

I tried to stay on the right side of the law

However I've been there

And I've seen how much money there is to be made on the
road
I felt my heart turning cold

I need hope

The future isn't looking so bright

I'm finding it hard to write and it's like

I've got no choice but to do wrong in order to live right

I need hope

Wherever you are

I'll find you

When I do

I'm never letting go

I'll see you soon

Hope

Henergy

Energy is powerful beyond measure

Emotions are the manifestation of energy of a particular
frequency and nature

Subject to transformations - ensure your emotions are the
product of positivity

Negative vibrations burn slow

Love

My Fashion Is Black

It is no longer fashionable to be black and speak of struggle

It is not the 1950's

We are not living in the 'dirty south'

We are no longer afraid of the ills of racial violence

We are no longer openly arrested for the words that leave our mouth

I am educated in a class of peers whose heritage spans the breadth of the western hemisphere and the length of the south

So where possibly could it be fashionable to speak of systematic racism?

Announcements of national demonstrations do not rile excitement across generations

The on sight beating and killing of black folk is no more common than celebrities speaking out against blatant cultural degradation

It is far from fashionable to be enraged by the dire depths of parliamentary misrepresentation

It is most certainly not fashionable to be Black and speak of the struggle

In an era where it remains of the highest fashion to be Black

If you ride upon the bandwagon all things Black

Talk of struggle must ride in the back

While all things niggerish and slack

Ride shot gun

Vernacular

And I am tired

I appreciate there are many things to be desired

Idols to be admired

But never at the cost of triumphs acquired by legends of yesteryear

Let it be written here

That the struggle was never meant to be fashionable

Never meant to be the epicentre of popular culture

Never meant to be the beacon of hope that babylon accepted to be more palatable for its tireless culture vulture

It is not fashionable to be Black and speak of the struggle

But it never was.

Long live the children of whom freedom awaits.

Free

Free flies the bird that flies alone

Where I choose to rest my head

Is where I choose to call my home

Free

Daddy's Going To Change The World

For this life, I used to pray

Now I wonder how to say

Baby listen, daddy can't stay

Daddy's going to change the world

Work begins today

The Walk Alone

The walk alone

Something I must do

Nobody will be there to back me or protect me from what lies ahead

I said

The walk alone

Is something I must do

Nonetheless I am prepared

My bags are packed, I have tied my boots

I am ready to embrace the world

Ready to see something new

The walk alone is something I must do

As a man

If I must I will if I will I can

Analyse prepare and plan

For this journey I must do alone

Destination X is still unknown

Though what is known

Is that I am going on a journey

The walk must be done alone

A good traveler is not content on arriving

For He or She has no set destination

Consequently I carry these thoughts

From nation to nation

In time I will find what I seek

Inner peace is a gift to the meek

Carried only by my heart and my feet

I accept my fate because

I am the master of my own destiny

Therefore I am no longer afraid to walk alone

Over standing that home is where the heart is

Ones soul is free to roam

Write Your Own Story.

Cheers & thanks.
Manners & respect.

Who Killed The Stereotype?

Officers we're looking for a male fitting the IC3 description

Suspect is believed to have been involved in a murder

Apprehend and contain at all costs

He is believed to be highly intelligent highly dangerous and a threat to society

So I warn you, proceed with fucking caution

Because this male does not inhale

Toxins created by a popular green plants

Developed by local horticulture experts near you

Nor does this male indulge

In the supposedly womanizing, high rolling, prison going, over saturated genre better known to the common folk as, Gangster Rap

This male - no longer is a frequent window shopper of JD

His choice of dress is no longer the produce of child slave labour

In dingy Indonesian sweatshops exploiting children for over 15 hours a day

Here what I say

Be wary in your approach

These male's mannerisms are not comparable to that of wild dogs

Or apes subject to cramped enclosures in climates alien while being fed a
pittance or just enough to maintain their existence

As once was thought to be the case

Eyewitnesses say the perpetrator is armed

He, has, a, belt

Unafraid to use it the suspect is considered a risk to our godforsaken ignorance

The use of such concealed weapon is an offence punishable by up to 30 seconds
hard struggle preceding any dying urges to urinate freely

Here what I say

Intelligence leads us to believe our man is now likely to be using the street suffix
Obie

Yes that's O.B.E

Further intelligence indicates this chap moves in one of the two major gangs
operating throughout the UK

BSc and BA respectively

With possible connections to higher ranking gang positions such as MSc or PhD

Praise be to G.O.D

This is one career bloody criminal

PC's, PCSO's, MP's, probation workers, youth workers, teachers and judges of
our era

Not forgetting school heads

The news is in

The truth is out

The stereotype is dead

Placed neatly on your desk will be a signed confession

Championed by yours truly

Images depicted in 'urban' culture, music and movies

Relayed in the peanut brains of the stupid

Have been erased

Controlled and backspaced

Thus the future of an entire generation saved

For, I

Yes, I

Have no remorse or shame

In confessing to the murder of stain history could not succeed in washing away

I have killed the stereotype

I dare you to take me away

W.O.R.D.S

Forgive me for I am mistaken

May the gods of cultural linguistics

That resideth in the mouths and tongues

Of daughter and son

Have mercy on me

For the power to harness language and employ its use

Is a gift reserved for the fortunate few

But you - do not understand

This is fine, I hold no qualm with you

For I do not understand the inner workings of jumbo jets

Yet - I still fly

I do not possess the skills of master craftsmanship

Yet I dine on handcrafted tables

And rest on settees drinking the finest masala tea
watching ITV on cable

Now do you see?

I know near nothing of micro circuitry

Like you know near nothing of words

There is no disrespect in the words I speak

For tis my duty

To explore and to seek

How I can better communicate with those who simply do not
speak the same language as me

This is not posh speak

This is communication beyond words

This is a feeling between beings

Excavating the true meaning

Of words uttered from here to the Queensland Region

This, is the reason

I am here

The reason I live, the reason I dream

I would die by loyalty to any stream of words I spew

Though admittedly, all I have is my word

What haveth you?

The Smiling Coast

You cannot destroy our spirit

For we are the children of Africa

Love is our religion

Creativity our freedom

Happiness our guide

Spirit our strength

You cannot down press those

Who have lived to see the beauty of Africa

They judge us by western standards

Confusing globalization with westernization

They say we are a developing country

I say we are world leading

In every sense that matters

Our levels of happiness are second to none

We appreciate life just as the flower appreciates the sun

We are united in our efforts for a greater Gambia

From the village of Juffereh to the strip in Senegambia From Kunteh Kenteh island the whole of West Africa

We are happy, we are free

We have the richest of history

As well as the brightest of futures

Which unlike our pre-enslavement past

Will not become a mystery

But last

Like footprints on the moon

Our impression on this world will endure long after we have come to pass

So when you think of us

Know that our struggle is temporary

Our passion is legacy

Where intolerance is sickness

Love will forever be our remedy

This is

We are

The Smiling Coast of Africa

Ode to MLK

50 years ago, a man had a dream

Expressed through a symphony of words

Decorated in pride - wreaking of pain

This dream came to be in the winter of 1929

The small town of Atlanta drenched in the tears of men, women and children
oppressed

Birthed a child

Raised a man

And the nightmare dirty south

Bought forth a good man with a dream

Prosperous, altruistic, amorous as well as powerful in nature

This dream would ignite the minds of men and women across the globe

From house Negro to free man

The fear of equality was driven deep out of the minds of those who fought so
hard to legislate their ignorance

"No blacks, no dogs, no Irish"

Became

No guns, no knives, and no fighting

Merely civil disobedience

Simple expressions of unhappiness

Fuck you

Fuck your politics

We as a people demand equality and by the grace of god we will be equal

Whether you are ready for it or not

50 years ago a man had a dream

His name was Martin Luther King

50 years later we're still dreaming

So hear the message I bring

I demand you to wake up, rise, hear the alarm bells ring

The dream is over

Today our future begins.

Madiba

If only the words existed to describe the life of our Madiba

How truly blessed our ears would be

Forgive me of my shortcomings in the delivery of this ode

I can provide no amazing analogies or awe-inspiring synonyms

To describe the ubiquitous nature of his influence

To live, to protest. to be imprisoned and then to be praised for your cause

Is a road few could have hoped to endure

I expect many of you anticipate a verse full of praise

Again, I disappoint

Forgive me but I shall explain

Madiba once said

'I was not a messiah but an ordinary man who had become a leader because of extraordinary circumstances'

What he was saying was

Madiba could have been you; Madiba could have been me

Madiba spoke up, for a nation in need

When freedom was stifled

His voice allowed it to breathe

He was no messiah

He was like you, he was like me

1962, a year of great change

Brazil won the World Cup, Maryln Monroe died, Jamaica gained
independence from the UK and Nelson Mandela was spent his first days inside

Unknown to the majority of the globe

It took the best part of 27 years for his stature to grow

Protest on protest

The calls for freedom echoed so hopeless

Political figures across the world divided by the subject

Could not have foreseen what was to happen next

Indeed, he was freed

Inauguration Day 1994, May 10th

Was inexplicably beautiful

A free South Africa

Not yet equal but on the righteous path to be so

Imagine making the transition from captive to hero

From activist to president without the slightest inflation of ego

Humble at heart

Steady with mind

Our Madiba lives on

Until the absence of time

'When a man has done what he conceives to be his duty to his people to his
country. He can rest in peace. I believe I have made that effort.'

Nelson Mandela

Boston 'The Orator' Williams